Presented to:

_____

From:

_____

Date:

_____

Fields *of* Abundance

COUNTRYMAN®

SIMPLE WORDS *of* WISDOM *to* RECEIVE
GOD'S BLESSINGS *for* YOUR EVERY NEED

God's Gift of Abundance

Introduction

Many of us are reluctant to ask God to bless us with abundance ... perhaps we have been raised to believe that God has bigger concerns in the world than our needs ... or that it is selfish to focus on what we want ... or that God helps those who help themselves ...

While it is true that God wants us to have a heart for the world, to be a cheerful giver, and to be a responsible worker, it is impossible to read God's Word without quickly realizing that He desires to bless His children—and assuredly, you are His child. He has promised us an abundance that is "beyond understanding." He has invited—and yes, commanded—us to bring our needs and requests before Him, to "ask" Him to bless us. Jesus told His disciples, ask and you will receive.

Could it be that if we understand God's abundance more clearly, we could better and more fully experience and share His blessings with others? As you reflect on the following pages, open your eyes and heart to the abundance that awaits you today.

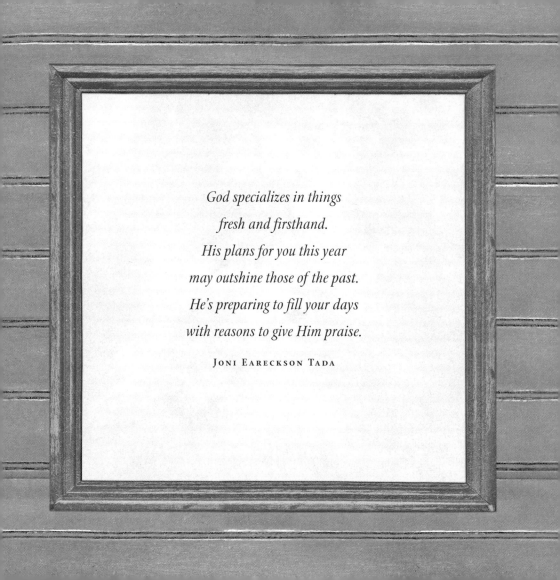

God specializes in things
fresh and firsthand.
His plans for you this year
may outshine those of the past.
He's preparing to fill your days
with reasons to give Him praise.

Joni Eareckson Tada

Abundance is God's *gift*
to His children—
and you are His child.

Abundance is much more
than material wealth.

Abundance is the rich
experience of friendship.

Abundance is a dazzling array
of glittering stars in an azure
night sky that stirs hearts
to wonder and awe.

Abundance is the profound
experience of knowing God.

We pray for sunshine every day—and when rain
doesn't fall, we wonder why our crops are parched
and small and our souls in need of cleansing.

Rather, ask God to grant you a spirit
to enjoy and savor all seasons and all days—
even when storm clouds burst.

We can learn much from watching a group
of children as they gleefully frolic in the rain
without a complaint in the world.

Prepare your soil. Plant your
seeds. Weed, water, and tend
the furrows of your garden.

But when you see that first
flash of glistening green
growth burst through the dark
brown soil, stop and thank
God. Your faithfulness and
work will be richly rewarded,
but only God can create the
miracle of life.

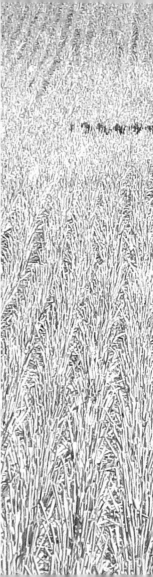

My life changed the day that I
realized with brilliant clarity
that God is good and kind and
truly wants to bless His
children. That awareness has
given me a sense of gratitude
that permeates my relationship
with God—and with others.
I have found appreciation to be
so much richer a way to think,
feel, and live. I can scarcely
believe that I was so easily
satisfied with my previous
thoughts of self-sufficiency,
avarice, and cynicism.

*Every good and perfect gift
is from above, and comes down
from the Father of lights,
with whom there is no variation
or shadow of turning.*

JAMES 1:17 NKJV

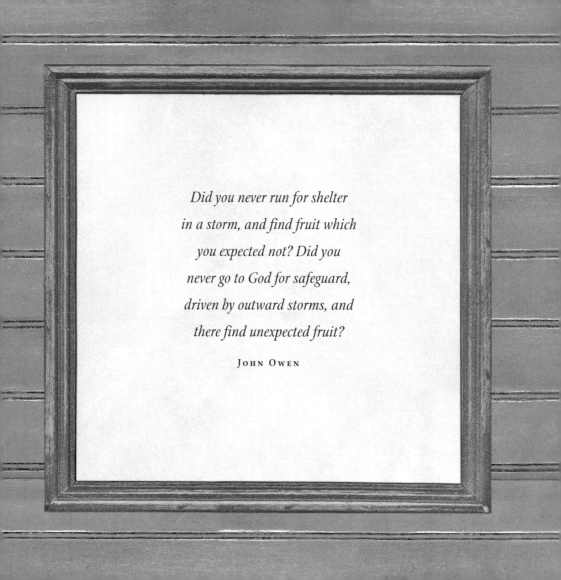

Did you never run for shelter
in a storm, and find fruit which
you expected not? Did you
never go to God for safeguard,
driven by outward storms, and
there find unexpected fruit?

JOHN OWEN

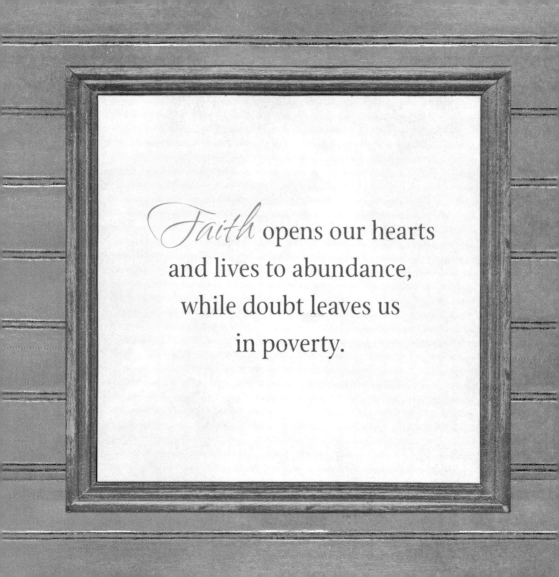

Faith opens our hearts
and lives to abundance,
while doubt leaves us
in poverty.

Right now, God is at work to bring about blessings in your life you can't even imagine. Even if you tried to imagine what God is up to, it is impossible to comprehend His ways, His plans, and even His sense of humor when blessing His children.

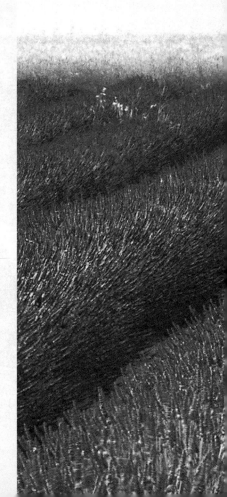

From the tiniest beginnings
come great and marvelous
works. Faith the size of a
mustard seed moves mountains.
And so God hides the mystery
and power of new life within
a tiny seed already planted
within your soul.

If your ship of fortune hasn't yet
sailed into harbor, you might
have to swim out to meet it.

Pursue your dreams with passion,
energy, and diligence. In other words,
live your life with faith.

God sees all circumstances
and knows how to orchestrate
perfect timing as He blesses you.
All He asks of you is to simply
trust Him as you live your
life unshackled by the
burden of fear.

What is faith?
It is the confident assurance
that what we hope for
is going to happen.
It is the evidence of things
we cannot yet see.

HEBREWS 11:1 NLT

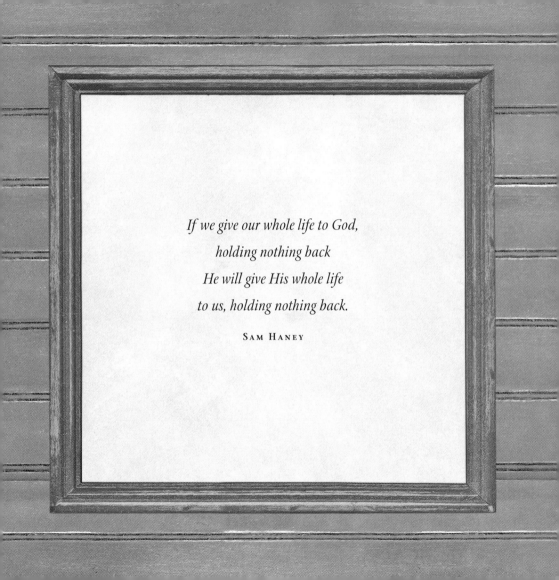

If we give our whole life to God,

holding nothing back

He will give His whole life

to us, holding nothing back.

SAM HANEY

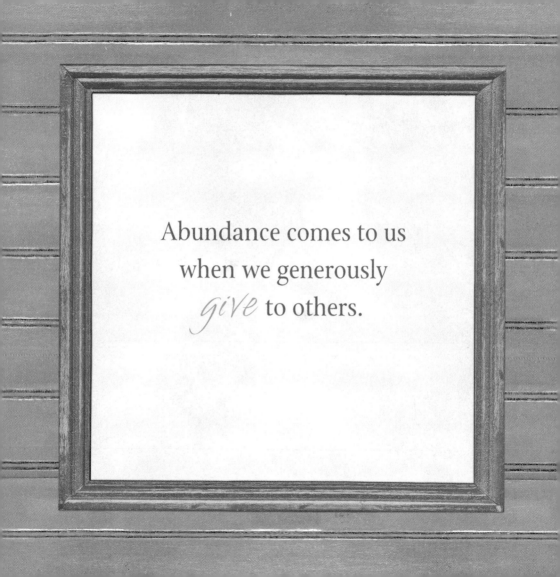

Abundance comes to us
when we generously
give to others.

Jesus taught that it is more blessed
to give than to receive.

Consider that it is only those who already possess
something who are able to share with others.

When you share from your abundance,
do so quietly and with all humility lest you
draw attention to yourself in a display
of pride or to the one who is in need.

The joy of giving from your own abundance
is all the reward your heart could ever want.

When you give generously—and cheerfully—a portion of your income, all that you have left goes so much further than when you spent it all on yourself.

Jesus did not multiply the loaves and fishes of those who hid their lunches for fear they might have to share with others. His miracle of multiplication was reserved for the young boy who opened his simple lunch sack— and his heart—to others.

Don't worry if someone you have been generous
with does not treat you in kind.

Keeping score and holding grudges only serves
to sully and shrink the spirit of a joyful giver.

Assuredly your generosity will be rewarded.

Trust God to determine the direction from which
the winds of grace blow into your life.
From whence, you know not, nor does it matter.

So when you give to the poor,
don't let anyone know what you
are doing. Your giving should
be done in secret. Your Father
can see what is done in secret,
and he will reward you.

MATTHEW 6:3-4

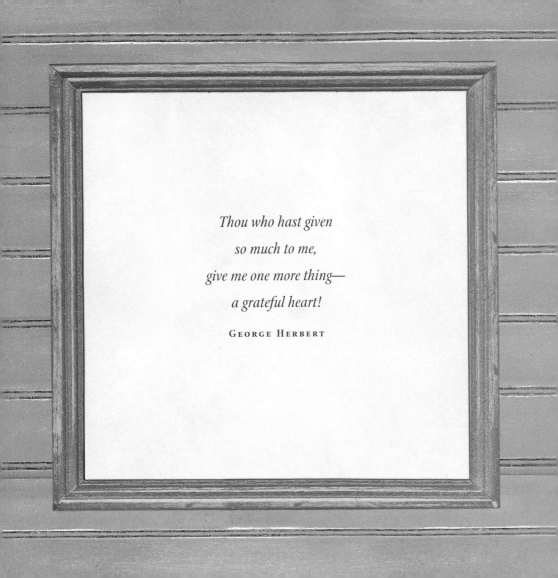

Thou who hast given
so much to me,
give me one more thing—
a grateful heart!

GEORGE HERBERT

We discover that
there is abundance
all around us when
we look at the world
with eyes of *gratitude.*

Thank You ...

Two powerful words

that enrich the spirit

of both speaker

and hearer.

Oftentimes abundance is more about our perspective than the number of things we own.

Whose life is richer? The poor man who appreciates his warm but tattered coat—or the wealthy man who is angry and resentful that his neighbor's car is newer than his own?

Gratitude begets a wealth of heart that can never be taken away.

Nothing will rob you
of your wealth more quickly
than the monster from the
pits of hell named Envy.

Draw the sword of content-
ment and slay that dragon
which would leave you a
pauper while living in the
King's castle.

What have you to be grateful
for? When you were sad, God
sent a comforter. When you
were sick, He was your healer.
When you were alone, He was
your friend. When you were
confused, He was your counselor
and guide. When your heart
was lost in sin, He sent
His Son to save you.

As parents we delight
in giving gifts to our children
because we love them and want to
bless their lives. Our delight is
doubled when we see their eyes—
and hearts—light up with joy.
Our delight is tripled when we
hear from their lips words
of gratitude and appreciation.

Our Heavenly Father delights in
blessing us, but His joy—and our
own joy at receiving His gifts—is
not complete until we express in
words our sincere thanks from
the depths of our hearts.

Now to Him who is able
to do exceedingly abundantly
above all that we ask or think,
according to the power
that works in us, to Him
be glory in the church
by Christ Jesus to all generations,
forever and ever. Amen.

Ephesians 3:20-21 NKJV

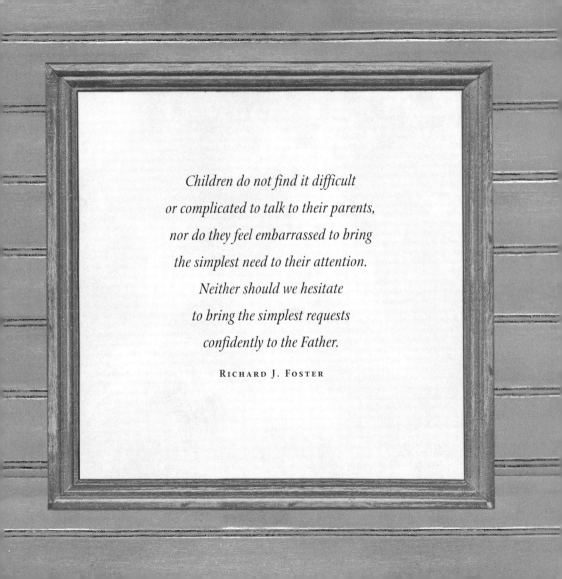

Children do not find it difficult
or complicated to talk to their parents,
nor do they feel embarrassed to bring
the simplest need to their attention.
Neither should we hesitate
to bring the simplest requests
confidently to the Father.

RICHARD J. FOSTER

God invites you to look
to Him for abundant and
extravagant blessings—
to simply *ask.*

Do you feel beset by a crush of debt and bills and too little income? Is a relationship in your life troubled?

Refuse to give in to despair. Now is your opportunity to see that God has always been with you; and He's waiting for you to turn to Him with faith and humility. He's waiting for you to ask Him for help!

To reap a great harvest
in the fall, the farmer must
plant the right seeds in
springtime. What seeds of
abundance have you planted
in the fields of your life?

Of course we don't give
merely to receive. But
in God's divine economy,
it is still ever so—when
we plant seeds of goodness,
our harvest awaits us.

59

God does not give
capriciously; if something
is taken away from you,
He'll replace it with
something better.
He loves to give good gifts
to His children.

And lest you doubt
or forget it, hear again,
you are God's child.

God knows your dreams
and the desires of your heart.
Nonetheless, He asks that we
pour out our hearts to Him and
take refuge in Him, seeking Him
for the things we most need.

*Yet you do not have
because you do not ask.*

JAMES 4:2 NKJV

Faith is not a storm cellar to which men

and women can flee for refuge

from the storms of life. It is, instead,

an inner force that gives them the strength

to face those storms and their

consequences with serenity of spirit.

SAM J. ERVIN, JR.

There are days of trial
when God grants a special
abundance of *spirit*
to His loved ones.

Even in the desert, streams
of God's living water flow.

If this is your season to wander alone
in the wilderness, be assured that you
will return to your village and loved ones
with a renewed sense of power and purpose.

Some of God's richest blessings
cannot be seen with the human eye.

Being God's child is a healthier, fuller, richer life than
any other—no matter what winds may blow your way.

If God can turn a tribal chieftain with no children
of his own into the father of many nations...

If God can use a stammering, reluctant outcast with
a murderous past to deliver a nation from slavery...

If God can use a simple peasant girl accused
of immorality to bear His son to the world...

Just think what He can do with you.

Hold onto the promise that God restores His people.

*"I know what I'm planning for you," says the Lord. "I have good plans
for you, not plans to hurt you. I will give you hope and a good future."*

Jeremiah 29:11

Dear Heavenly Father,

Thank You so much for Your many blessings. Open my eyes today, Lord, and help me see the ways You've blessed me. Give me a heart of gratitude, O God, and remind me of Your goodness and lovingkindness.

Lord, I pray for Your continued provision today. I lift my needs to You knowing that You lavish grace on Your children. Thank You, Lord, for being all I need—and so much more.

Amen.

For the past 12 years, Green Hill Productions has been the leader in creating music from quality instrumentals to exclusive compilations of legendary artists for all of our customers to enjoy. To find out more about our products or to locate a store near you, contact us at 1 (800) 972-5900 or check us out on the internet at www.greenhillmusic.com. Thanks to our valued partnership with Thomas Nelson, it is a pleasure to offer our music for your listening pleasure. Enjoy and have an inspiring read!

Sam Levine has given color and expression to a wide variety of artists' tracks, including Amy Grant, the Neville Brothers, Vince Gill and Michael McDonald.

Sam has more than 10 artist CD's in the smooth jazz and contemporary Christian genres. He has been nominated three times for a Dove Award and played on at least two Grammy Award winning recordings.

Sam continues to be an active studio musician, but he also leads a band called "City Lights" that is popular for wedding receptions and business conventions.

Violinist **David Davidson** has performed around the world as concertmaster, soloist, and chamber musician. Currently, David is the concertmaster of The Tennessee Summer Symphony and The Nashville Chamber Orchestra. He's also a member of The Nashville String Machine, the prestigious studio orchestra that records for the most major artists in the Nashville music community.

David's passionate violin playing can be heard on the hugely successful hymns projects by Michael W. Smith and recordings by Twila Paris and Third Day.

GREEN HILL
PRODUCTIONS